The Human Body

The Nervous System

CHECKERBOARD SCIENCE LIBRARY

THE HUMAN BODY

Kristin Petrie MS, RD • ABDO Publishing Company

visit us at
www.abdopublishing.com

Published by ABDO Publishing Company, 4940 Viking Drive, Edina, Minnesota 55435.
Copyright © 2007 by Abdo Consulting Group, Inc. International copyrights reserved in all
countries. No part of this book may be reproduced in any form without written permission from
the publisher. The Checkerboard Library™ is a trademark and logo of ABDO Publishing
Company.

Printed in the United States.

Cover Photo: Corbis
Interior Photos: Corbis pp. 1, 4, 5, 11, 12, 13, 18, 20, 21, 23, 24, 25, 27, 29; Getty Images p. 26;
    © M.Dauenheimer/Custom Medical Stock Photo p. 19; Peter Arnold pp. 8, 17; Visuals
    Unlimited pp. 7, 9, 14

Series Coordinator: Heidi M. Dahmes
Editors: Heidi M. Dahmes, Megan Murphy
Art Direction: Neil Klinepier

Library of Congress Cataloging-in-Publication Data

Petrie, Kristin, 1970-
    The nervous system / Kristin Petrie.
        p. cm. -- (The human body)
    Includes index.
    ISBN-10 1-59679-712-6
    ISBN-13 978-1-59679-712-3
    1. Nervous system--Juvenile literature. I. Title.

QP361.5.P48 2006
612.8--dc22
                                                    2005048321

CONTENTS

Supercomputer

How do you remember the words to your favorite song? Why do you flinch when something is thrown at you? How do you chew gum and walk at the same time? Your nervous system allows all of these things to happen.

The nervous system is the control center for your entire body. It is smarter than any computer. In fact, you could call it your supercomputer. Your supercomputer **coordinates** all of your body's actions and reactions.

Your brain is a bit different from a computer. For example, when parts of your brain are damaged, memories still exist. But, when part of a computer's "memory" is destroyed, nothing is left.

Your supercomputer is made of two parts. They are the central nervous system (CNS) and the peripheral nervous system (PNS). The CNS is made up of your brain and spinal cord. The spinal cord connects your brain to the PNS. The PNS contains all the other nerves in your body. These include the nerves in your nose down to the nerves in your toes!

The brain and nervous system work together to keep your body going. This team makes your heart beat. It keeps you breathing without thinking about it. It allows you to see and read these words. And, it helps you turn the page.

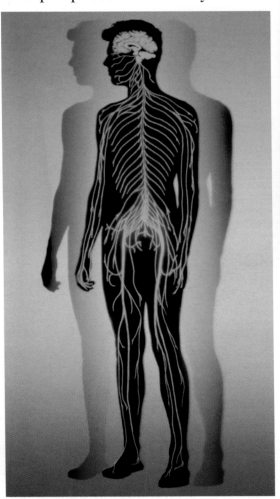

Your brain uses your many nerves to send messages throughout your body.

YOUR COMMANDER

The brain is your supercomputer's commander. When you're all grown up, your commander will weigh about 48 ounces (1,361 g). A dog's brain weighs about two and a half ounces (71 g). A cat's brain only weighs about one ounce (28 g). No wonder you are the master!

You have probably seen a brain on television. It's not pretty. The brain looks like a squishy, grayish blob with lots of folds. The many wrinkles add to your brain's surface area.

The brain is made of several parts. The cerebrum is the largest. It is the part with all the wrinkles. The cerebrum is responsible for thinking. It allows you to remember what day it is. It helps you with your spelling. And, it reminds you to say please and thank you.

The cerebrum is made up of two halves. The right half controls the left side of your body. It is in charge of your creative thinking. You use it when listening to music and picking colors. The cerebrum's left side controls the right side of your body. The left half helps you with **logical** thinking. It helps you do things like math.

Another important part of the cerebrum is the motor area. The motor area runs across the top of your cerebrum. It controls your voluntary muscles. These are the muscles that move when you want them to. Thank your motor area when you turn this page!

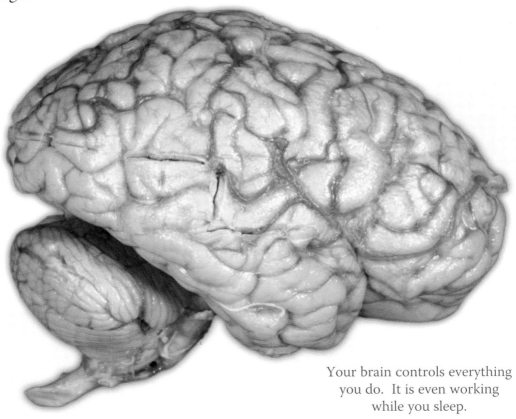

Your brain controls everything you do. It is even working while you sleep.

LITTLE BRAIN

The cerebellum is another important part of your brain. In Latin, *cerebellum* means "little brain." It is much smaller than the cerebrum. The cerebellum sits below and behind the cerebrum.

Despite its small size, the cerebellum's job is huge. The cerebellum gives you balance and **coordination**. It works hard to help you walk, run, and spin. Thank your little brain when you dance to your favorite song.

Below the cerebrum and in front of the cerebellum is your brain stem. This small part connects your brain to your spinal cord. It acts like your brain's secretary. The brain stem sorts and delivers the millions of messages sent between your brain and your body.

Without the nervous system telling you what to do, your muscles would be useless. You wouldn't even be able to breathe.

The brain stem also has another important job. It controls the body's involuntary muscles. Involuntary muscles do things like make your heart beat. They help you **digest** your lunch. And, they keep you breathing. These functions are all necessary to keep your body running properly!

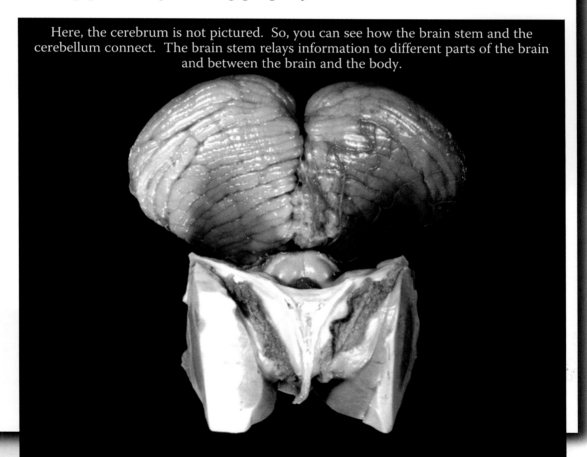

Here, the cerebrum is not pictured. So, you can see how the brain stem and the cerebellum connect. The brain stem relays information to different parts of the brain and between the brain and the body.

REGULATORS

The brain contains other parts with interesting names and cool jobs. The hippocampus is the part of your cerebrum that helps you remember things. Did you leave your house key in the refrigerator? Your hippocampus will remind you where to look for it.

Did you fall out of a tree when you were little? Your hippocampus helps you remember that, too. With its help, we have short- and long-term memory.

The pituitary gland is another tiny part of your brain with a huge job. If you've outgrown yet another pair of shoes, thank your pituitary gland. This gland sends growth **hormones** through your body. It sits front and center in your brain.

Just behind the pituitary gland is the hypothalamus. Think of the hypothalamus as your body's thermostat. If you're cold, it tells your body to shiver. If you're hot, it makes you sweat. Your hypothalamus keeps your body at the right temperature.

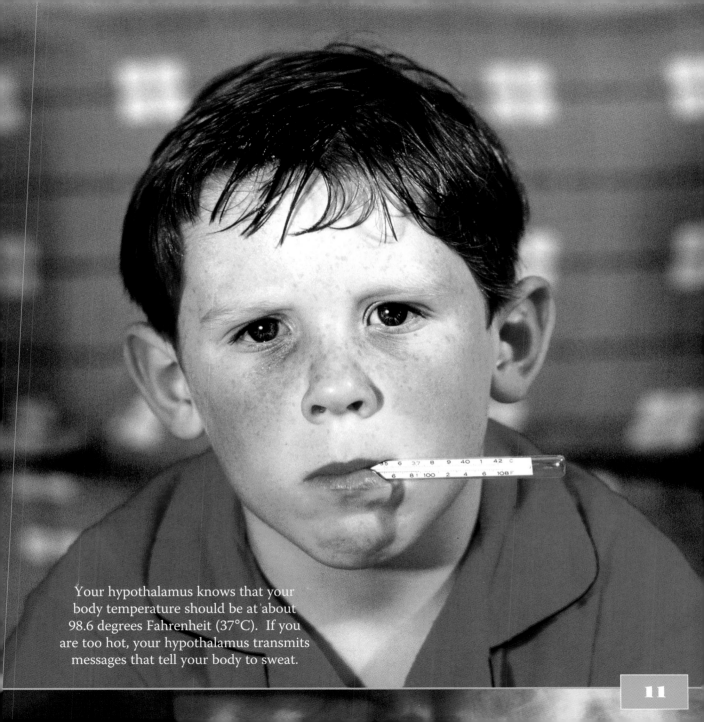

Your hypothalamus knows that your body temperature should be at about 98.6 degrees Fahrenheit (37°C). If you are too hot, your hypothalamus transmits messages that tell your body to sweat.

THE SPINAL CORD

The spinal cord connects your brain to the rest of your body. This "cord" is actually a bundle of nerves. The bundle is about as wide as your finger.

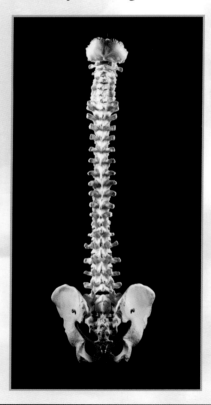

The spinal cord starts at the brain stem and runs about two-thirds of the way down the spine. Reach your hand around and feel the bumps of your backbone. The spinal cord lies safely inside.

The spinal cord sends messages to and from the brain. For example, let's say you want to write your name. Your brain sends a message down your spinal cord. Next, the message travels to your arm and fingers. Once there,

The spinal column holds the spinal cord in place.

motor nerves move the muscles in your fingers. Then, you write your name.

Your brain isn't the only body part that can send out messages. Sensory nerves also send information to the brain for decoding. For example, nerves in your fingers can send messages to your brain. If you touch an ice cube, your brain gets a message. That's cold!

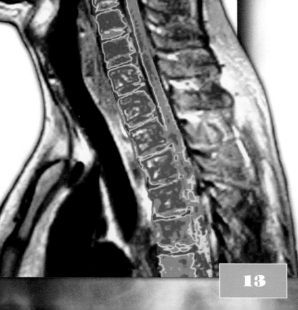

The spinal cord contains nerves that branch off to every body part. An adult's spinal cord is about .4 inches (1 cm) in diameter and about 16.5 to 18 inches (42 to 46 cm) long.

NERVE CELLS

The spinal cord and the brain are made up of millions of nerve cells, or neurons. These cells come in many different sizes. Some are short and pass messages from one cell to the next. Others are very long. Some reach all the way to your big toe!

There are three parts to every nerve cell. The cell body has a nucleus that contains **genetic** information. It also has fluid called cytoplasm, which contains mitochondria that produce energy.

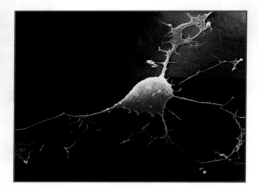

This human neuron shows the axons and the dendrites branching off of the cell body.

The second part of the nerve cell is the dendrites. Dendrites are thin "branches" that come off of the cell body. Dendrites are usually very short. A neuron may have a few or very many dendrites. Their job is to bring information to the cell body.

Axons also branch off of the cell body. Some axons are short and connect to the next neuron. Other axons are very long.

These axons stretch all the way to your muscles. All axons take information away from the cell body.

Axons are surrounded by a fatty material called myelin. Myelin protects the axon. It also helps nerve signals travel quickly from one cell to the next.

A NEURON

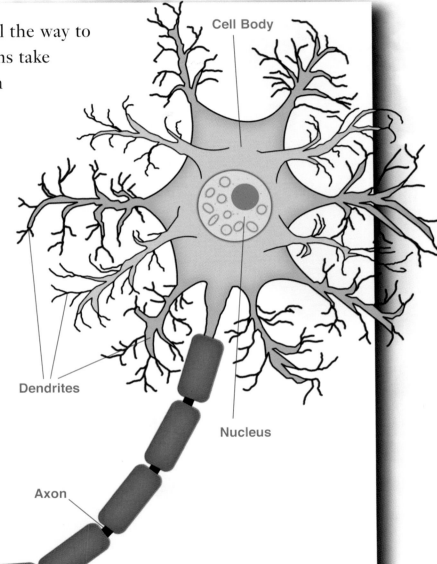

Cell Body

Dendrites

Nucleus

Myelin Sheath

Axon

ELECTRICITY, IN MY BRAIN?

Nerve impulses get around so quickly. It seems easy! However, messages must find a way to get across a small gap between each nerve cell. This gap between neurons is called a synapse.

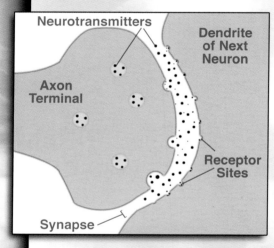

A synapse separates one neuron's axons from another's dendrites. Chemicals called neurotransmitters help messages cross that gap.

When a nerve signal reaches the end of an axon, the axon releases a chemical into the synapse. The chemical allows the message to jump across the gap. When the message reaches the next nerve cell, an electrical shock happens. The shock helps speed the message to its next destination.

Here is an example of how pain messages travel. Even if you are an expert bike rider, let's say you fall.

As you hit the ground, nerve endings in your skin pick up a signal. This signal shoots through your dendrites to the axon.

The signal then reaches the gap between the axon and the dendrite it is targeting. A chemical allows the signal to jump across the synapse.

At the next nerve cell, an electrical impulse keeps the message going. The signal speeds along, like

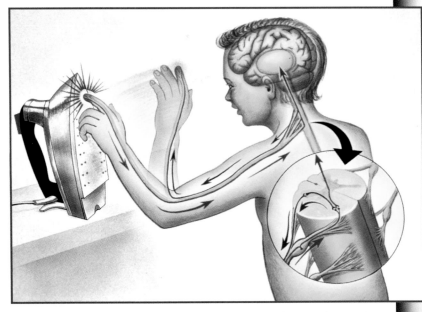

The red arrows show how pain signals travel to a person's brain. The green arrows show the reaction sent by the spinal cord.

dominoes falling. At the CNS, the message reaches your brain. The brain decodes the message. Pain!

THE SENSES

Different types of nerves send different messages around your body. Sensory nerves are particularly important. They gather information from the world around you. Things you see, hear, feel, smell, and taste become messages. These messages travel in your nervous system.

Sensory nerves carry messages from your sense organs, such as your ears and eyes, to your brain for processing. Or, they may skip your brain and travel just to your spinal cord and then to your muscles.

Vision is the primary sense for most humans.

Your brain processes sensory signals and tells your body how to react. Your muscles then respond to your brain's instructions. Your nose muscles might scrunch up at a bad smell. If you hear a loud noise, you could turn your head to see what it is. When you taste something sweet, you might smile. If you pet a frog, you may cringe at the slimy feeling.

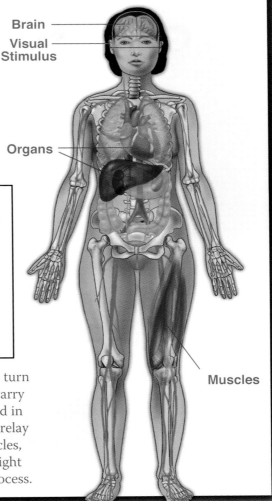

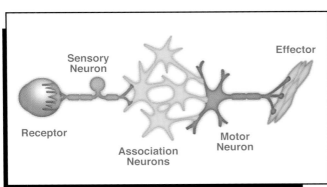

In the diagram above, the eye contains receptors that turn information into nerve impulses. Sensory neurons carry the impulses to association neurons, which are found in the brain and the spinal cord. Then, motor neurons relay instructions from the brain to the effectors, or muscles, organs, and other body parts. The diagram to the right shows all of the body parts involved in this speedy process.

REFLEXES

To check your DTR, a doctor taps on your patellar tendon. This tapping stretches the tendon and the thigh muscle that is connected to it.

Sometimes our muscles have a life of their own. If a frog suddenly jumped at you, you would jump too! This ultrafast and unplanned movement is a reflex. Reflexes are involuntary, or automatic, responses. They protect your body from harm. Blinking and coughing are examples of reflexes.

We also have conditioned reflexes. Does your mouth water when you see your favorite food? This is a conditioned reflex. When we are used to something, our body reacts automatically.

Another reflex you have is the deep **tendon** reflex (DTR). When the doctor taps your knee and your leg kicks out, that is a DTR. The **tendon** below your knee shoots a message to your spinal cord. Your spinal cord shoots one back. Then, your lower leg pops up. The message completely skips your brain.

Coughing clears your airways of bothersome things.

LEARNING

Your nervous system contains millions of neurons. You were born with all of the nerve cells you will ever have. But at first, many were not connected to each other. Neurons become connected through the repetition of actions.

Everyone learns things through practice. Your brain learns the same way. As you learn, messages travel between certain neurons over and over again. Eventually, the brain builds pathways between these neurons. This is how things become easier, and you can do them faster.

As you grow older, you learn more difficult things. Remember that great day when you first rode a bike? Your brain shot messages to and from many areas. These messages told you to pedal, steer, stay upright, and look where you're going! That's a lot of information to send back and forth. Luckily, your brain etched new pathways. Now bike riding is easy.

Opposite page: As you practice riding your bike, you create pathways between certain neurons. So, you won't have to relearn how to ride your bike every time you get on it.

PROBLEMS

Certain diseases cause the nervous system to function improperly. In multiple sclerosis (MS) sufferers, the **insulation** around many axons is missing. The nerves are not protected. So, they cannot conduct impulses as well as those that are insulated. People with MS may have difficulty walking and seeing.

Epilepsy is another **disorder** of the nervous system. Victims suffer from muscle **convulsions**. These convulsions happen

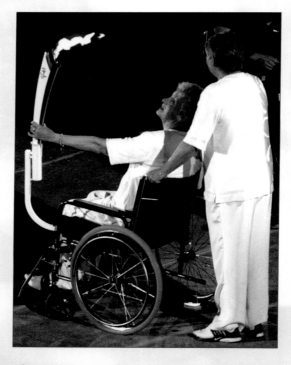

Former Australian Olympic gold medalist Betty Cuthbert learned in 1981 that she had MS. Since then, she has spent much of her time raising funds for MS research.

Research is HOPE

Television talk show host Montel Williams has MS. The Montel Williams MS Foundation funds research to work toward a cure.

when neurons in the brain fire off an unusual amount of impulses. This results in a **seizure**. Luckily, medications can reduce the severity of this **disorder**.

Brain and spinal cord injuries can also affect the nervous system. Injuries can happen in car and bike crashes, sports, and playground accidents. Unfortunately, these injuries are all too common.

A bad crash or a blow to the head can give you a concussion. Concussions happen when the brain knocks against the skull. When the brain is knocked around, it can't function properly.

Most people return to normal after a mild concussion. But, a severe concussion may cause problems with memory, concentration, and dizziness.

Actor Christopher Reeve damaged his spinal cord in a horseback-riding accident in 1995. Reeve was paralyzed as a result of the accident.

Injury to your spinal cord can be tragic. You may lose the use of body parts. This is called paralysis. An injury low on your spinal cord may cause you to lose the use of your legs. A high injury may cause paralysis from your neck down.

Now you know how valuable your nervous system is. Treat it right! Protect your spinal cord and your brain. Wear your seat belt properly. Never dive into unfamiliar water. When playing, always look before you leap. And wear a helmet when skateboarding, in-line skating, or riding your bike.

Fastening your seat belt is important for your safety. If you are wearing your seat belt during an accident, you are less likely to be injured.

FUEL

Your nervous system needs your help to work properly. The food you eat provides important **nutrients**. The nutrients from that peanut butter and jelly sandwich you ate are working hard right now.

Let's break it down. The bread provides **glucose**, the brain's favorite fuel. The peanut butter provides fat and protein. Fat helps make myelin, which is the coating on your nerves. Protein produces chemicals that keep those nerve impulses moving.

Vitamins and minerals play important roles, too. Vitamin A plays a large role in your vision. The mineral calcium is needed for the proper **transmission** of electrical impulses. The smooth transmission of these impulses is important in everything you do.

To help your nervous system stay healthy, eat a balanced diet. This means you should eat a moderate amount of many kinds of foods. Also, let your brain rest by getting enough sleep. And finally, don't drink alcohol, take drugs, or use tobacco. These substances will prevent your nervous system from being its best!

Take good care of your body, and in turn it will function properly. Eat healthy foods and stay active.

GLOSSARY

convulsion – a violent and involuntary contraction or series of contractions of the muscles.

coordination – the united functioning of parts.

digest – to break down food into substances small enough for the body to absorb.

disorder – a physical or mental illness.

genetic – of or relating to the branch of biology that deals with the principles of heredity.

glucose – a simple sugar existing in plants and in the blood of humans and animals.

hormone – a chemical messenger that helps regulate activities in the body.

insulation – material used to prevent the transfer of heat, electricity, or sound.

logical – of or relating to sound thinking or reason.

nutrient – a substance found in food and used in the body to promote growth, maintenance, and repair.

seizure – a sudden attack of a disease.

tendon – a band of tough fibers that joins a muscle to another part, such as a bone.

transmission – the act of sending from one person or place to another.

SAYING IT

cerebellum - sehr-uh-BEH-luhm

cerebrum - suh-REE-bruhm

cytoplasm - SEYE-tuh-pla-zuhm

hippocampus - hih-puh-KAM-puhs

hypothalamus - heye-poh-THA-luh-muhs

mitochondria - meye-tuh-KAHN-dree-uh

peripheral - puh-RIH-fuh-ruhl

pituitary - puh-TOO-uh-tehr-ee

sclerosis - skluh-ROH-suhs

synapse - SIH-naps

WEB SITES

To learn more about the nervous system, visit ABDO Publishing Company on the World Wide Web at www.abdopub.com. Web sites about the human body are featured on our Book Links page. These links are routinely monitored and updated to provide the most current information available.

INDEX